FENG-SHUI

THE ART OF IMPROVING YOUR HOME
TO ENHANCE YOUR LIFE

4	9	2
3	5	7
8	1	6

JONATHAN DEE

CE
CAXTON EDITIONS

Dedication

To Russell Morgan for his inscrutable help and advice

First published in the UK in 1999 by
Caxton Editions
16 Connaught Street
Marble Arch
London W2 2AF

ISBN: 1-84067-086-X

This is a MARS book

Edited, designed and produced by Haldane Mason, London
Editorial Director: Sydney Francis
Art Director: Ron Samuel
Editor: Jo-Anne Cox
Designer: Zoë Mellors
Picture Research: Jo-Anne Cox

Printed in China

Picture Acknowledgements

Robert Harding: Brock Photography back cover (centre left), 43, 51; Michael Brockway back cover (top right); Jean Brooks 10 (centre right), 12 (above centre); Ian Griffiths 7, 10 (bottom left), 12 (below centre); Robert Harding 6, 29, 34-35; Gavin Hellier 5; IPC Magazines front cover (far right), 37, 46, 47, 50, 62-63; David Lomax 10 (top), 12 (top); John Miller 10 (bottom right), 12 (centre); Photri 10 (centre left), 12 (bottom); **Haldane Mason:** 38-39, 40 (left); **Elizabeth Whiting & Associates:** front cover (far left), (centre left), (centre right), 19, 22, 23, 24, 27, 40-41, 54, 55, 61

Every effort has been made to trace the copyright holders and we apologize in advance for any unintentional omissions. We would be pleased to insert the appropriate acknowledgement in any subsequent edition of this publication.

Contents

What is *Feng-Shui?*

***Feng-shui* (which means 'Wind and Water') is an ancient oriental art designed to promote good health, happiness, prosperity, energy and enthusiasm through the correct placement of objects and appropriate decor. Its objective is to create an overall sense of harmony in a person's home and, therefore, their life.**

Feng-shui is an ancient practice in many oriental cultures. Much of the landscape of China, for example, has been shaped by human hands following the principles of *feng-shui* to complement the energies of Heaven and Earth. Indeed, some of the greatest monuments in the world, such as the Forbidden City of Peking and the Great Wall of China, were constructed with many of its principles in mind.

However, *feng-shui* practices are not some dimly remembered superstition left over from the lost days of Imperial China. Indeed, its influence is still very much alive today in places such as Singapore and Hong Kong. For example, several powerful financial institutions in these cities, such as the HSBC bank, pay enormous sums of money to respected *feng-shui* masters to ensure that their premises are in tune with the forces of Heaven and Earth and thus increase their prosperity.

In the Western world, too, *feng-shui* is becoming more and more popular and is widely adhered to by a significant amount of people. A word of warning, one can go to a great deal of expense consulting a *feng-shui* expert, who then baffles you with science and tells you, enigmatically, to move a sofa, ensure a set of curtains are kept closed or to add a plant

The winding Great Wall of China was thought to create chi *for the whole country.*

to a particular corner! In essence, however, the main principles of *feng-shui* are based on commonsense as you will discover as you read through this book and become more familiar with the concept.

The Main Aims of *Feng-shui*

In our busy lives it is often easy to forget that we are all children of nature and that our relationship with the world as a whole is part and parcel of our inner spirituality. This basic truth is integral to the Chinese art of *feng-shui* because, although it may seem obvious to point out, people can be profoundly affected by their immediate surroundings, both negatively and positively. *Feng-shui* aims to ensure that only positive states of mind and good fortune are created within your own personal environment.

Feng-shui has many different forms and several distinct traditions have grown over the centuries. This book will serve as an introduction to the art of *feng-shui,* helping you to improve your living conditions and hopefully to improve your life as well.

Understanding the Principles

Although much of *feng-shui* is concerned with the natural features of the landscape and the setting of a particular dwelling or business, this book concentrates on the interior of a home and the correct arrangement of the features of a home. Thus, the effect of the changes will be more immediate in your life.

Because there are several stages to understand and work through before you can assess your home and decide what changes need to be made, *feng-shui* may, at first, seem to be a very complicated business. However, this is not the case and you'll soon get the hang of it if you simply start at the beginning and work your way through.

Remember that if you do discover a problem in your home environment, there are some simple *feng-shui* remedies detailed throughout the book which will guide you and help to put things right without involving any major expense or extensive reconstruction work.

A statue of a protective dragon will help to ward off evil.

For example, in most cases the simple rearrangement of furniture or the addition of a mirror, a plant or a wind-chime into certain areas of the home will serve to harmonize your environment. You will find that with a little redecoration here and there or the simple task of moving a rug can work wonders!

As soon as you put some of the suggestions in this book into effect you will begin to feel a difference. Tradition states that it can take up to twenty-eight days (one lunar cycle) before any real effect can be felt, but I have tended to notice an immediate improvement especially when using a *Pa Kua* mirror (which is supplied with this book).

Above all you must bear in mind that *feng-shui* is an intuitive art in which a sense of harmony is all-important. You will probably find that the way you have decorated your home is already basically correct according to the rules of *feng-shui,* simply because you have been unconsciously in tune with your environment all along. If that's the case then all that will be required are a few minor adjustments here and there to bring yourself and your

A combination of straight lines and curves creates harmony in this complex.

home into complete harmony. *Feng-shui* becomes even more important if you have been feeling despondent because it may be that you are reacting adversely to some element in your surroundings which is disturbing you on an unconscious level.

Feng-shui is by no means an idealistic theory. On the contrary, its practical benefits have been proven over and over again for many centuries, and you too can apply its principles to improve your home and life. Read this book thoroughly, experiment with the *Pa Kua* mirror and lucky coins provided and see for yourself what an amazing difference *feng-shui* can make to your lifestyle.

Chi & the Opposites

***Feng-shui* is based on the movement of *chi* or more properly *sheng chi,* otherwise known as 'universal breath' or 'the energy of life'. This force flows through the universe, the earth and the human body. *Chi* brings good fortune in the form of physical energy, relationship affinity and material prosperity, so it is important to have a good flow of *chi* through your home.**

If *chi* is not allowed to flow freely around the home then it stagnates and transforms into destructive energy, known as *sha chi* or *sha.* This negative energy can cause bad luck, depression, loss of health and prosperity.

Chi is said to gently flow along curved lines while the 'doom laden' *sha chi* strikes like a 'secret arrow' along straight lines. This is the reason that oriental gardens rarely include straight lines in their design. Sharp corners, too, can create 'secret arrows' or 'noxious rays' which can harm your luck.

In oriental philosophy everything that lives contains *chi,* and *chi* has two sets of opposite yet complementary qualities, known as *yin* and *yang.*

The Opposites

Yang is an active, masculine, positive force, while *yin* is feminine, negative and passive. However, this does not mean that because of these properties *yang* should be regarded as being 'good' and *yin* 'bad', in fact, this view would be a gross distortion. Instead, remember that like day and night and summer and winter, *yin* and *yang* are part of a great cycle.

The ancient Chinese went even further than this by stating that *yin* contains the seeds of its opposite, *yang,* within itself, and vice versa. In fact, *yin* and *yang* are always expressed in ideas that include them both as complementary opposites. So when we feel good about ourselves, or our place in the world, our home or indeed any other place in which we feel happy, the *yin* and *yang* are considered to be in perfect balance. It is the main aim of *feng-shui* to ensure that this balance is constantly maintained, so that peace and harmony exists.

The box below lists some of the concepts associated with the paired opposites of *yin* and *yang*. Incidentally, this list could be continued until it contained every opposite in the universe.

Of course, *yin* and *yang* are not the only concepts we have to become familiar with to practice the principles of *feng-shui* because *yin* and *yang* operate through 'agents of change', better known as the Five Elements: Water, Wood, Fire, Earth and Metal (see pages 10–13).

THE MAIN PROPERTIES OF *YIN* AND *YANG*

Yang	*Yin*
Male	Female
Light	Dark
Hot	Cold
Hard	Soft
Light	Heavy
Positive	Negative
Heaven	Earth
Fire	Water
Mountain	Valley
Sharp	Blunt
Right	Left
Up	Down
Front	Back
Spirit	Body
Solid	Empty
Angular	Curved
Odd Numbers	Even Numbers
Moving	Static

This is the symbol of **Tai Chi**, *meaning the 'balance of the universe'.*

THE FIVE ELEMENTS & THE CREATIVE CYCLE

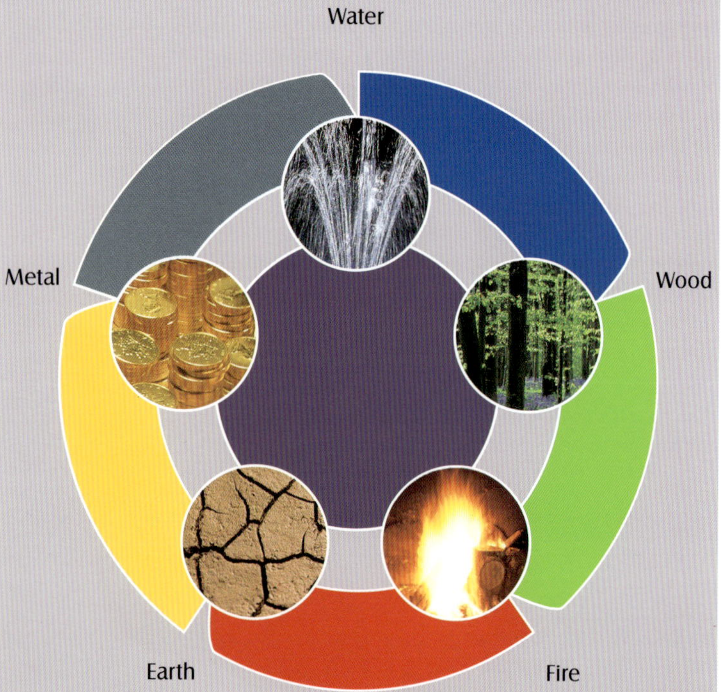

The Creative Cycle works in the following way:

Water feeds Wood
Wood fuels Fire
Fire creates Earth (in the form of ash)
Earth creates Metal
Metal can flow like Water

The Five Elements

Much of *feng-shui* is concerned with the relationships between the forces of nature, which are symbolized by the Five Elements, or *Wu-Xing*.

In Western tradition there are said to be four Elements: Earth, Air, Fire and Water, but for the Chinese who generally favour the lucky number five, they are Wood *(Mu)*, Fire *(Huo)*, Earth *(T'u)*, Metal *(Chin)* and Water *(Shui)*. They do not believe that the universe is literally made up of these materials, but that they represent States of Change – one constantly creating the next in the sequence.

The Creative Cycle

Beginning with the Water Element, the sequence of the Creative Cycle (see diagram, opposite) is as follows:

Water feeds Wood
Wood fuels Fire
Fire creates Earth (in the form of ash)
Earth creates Metal
Metal can flow like Water

The Destructive Cycle

However, the Elements bring dangers, too, because if the next stage in the creative sequence is missing then the cycle will become one of destruction.

Water quenches Fire
Fire melts Metal
Metal cuts Wood
Wood exhausts Earth
Earth pollutes Water

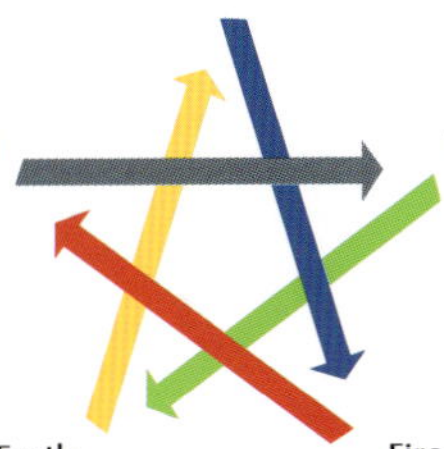

The Destructive Cycle

The Elements & Directions

Each Element is associated with a compass Direction (see box, right), therefore your home will be governed by one main Element (indicated by the Direction of your front door, see page 24), but it will also have all the other Elements distributed about the house or apartment (see pages 16–19).

Water governs the North
Wood governs the East and South East
Fire governs the South
Earth governs the Centre, the North East and the South West
Metal governs the West and North West

THE FIVE ELEMENTS & THEIR ASSOCIATIONS

Element	Symbolic Colours	Direction	Image	Shape
Water 	Black, Deep Blue	North	Tortoise 	Wavy Lines
Wood 	Green, Light Blue	East South East	Dragon 	Rectangle
Fire 	Red, Purple	South	Phoenix 	Triangle
Earth 	Yellow	Centre North East South West	Emperor 	Square
Metal 	White, Metallic tints	West North West	Tiger 	Circle, Oval

The Five Elements can be helpful if they are in harmony (see The Creative Cycle, pages 10–11) or troublesome if they are in conflict (see The Destructive Cycle, page 11). For example, the kitchen, which is governed by Fire and Water, can be harmful to health and prosperity if these two Elements, which are part of the Destructive Cycle (Fire quenches Water, see page 11), aren't made harmonious by the introduction of the Element Wood which lies between them in the Creative Cycle.

Similarly, this is the reason that having a bathroom in the middle of the home isn't a good idea. The bathroom is governed by the Water Element, so if it is positioned in the centre of the home it would be ruled by the Earth Element. Since Water and Earth are in conflict in the Destructve Cycle (Earth pollutes Water, see page 11), the addition of Metal is necessary to restore the balance.

So, we can deduce that if there is an Elemental conflict the solution lies in adding another Element which will harmonize the warring factions.

If Water conflicts Fire, add Wood
If Wood conflicts Metal, add Water
If Wood conflicts Earth, add Fire
If Fire conflicts Metal, add Earth
If Earth conflicts Water, add Metal

Using the Elements

Apart from governing compass Directions, the Five Elements also have symbolic colours, images and shapes associated with them (see page 12).

For example, if you were having trouble in the Metal sector of your home (West or North West), possibly because you had a fireplace or stove there (both are ruled by Fire), then the addition of a square, yellow rug would symbolize the Earth Element and harmonize the affected area. It would not be a good idea to add more of the Metal or Fire Elements, such as red, white, triangular or circular objects, because that would only emphasize the original imbalance.

Of course, this example is only one solution. *Feng-shui* is constrained only by the creative imagination. A stone might be placed in the affected Metal sector with equal effect, as could painting the whole area yellow or adding any object which suggests the Element Earth.

So, in essence, it is easy to change negative, destructive forces into harmonious and positive ones with a little Elementary thinking.

To complicate matters further, you too will have a ruling Element which may or may not be in tune with your home. To assess this, we will need to work out your Lucky Star Number.

Your Star Number

By working out your personal Star Number, you will discover the Element that is most fortuitous for you. In addition, it will also reveal your lucky and unlucky Directions and a suitable choice of colour co-ordinates that are most auspicious for your home.

Star Numbers are a branch of Chinese astrology and, like the more familiar 'Animal Signs' of the zodiac, are dependent on your year of birth.

To work out your Star Number, first check if you were born before the change of the Chinese New Year: this officially falls on the 4 February, but can vary quite a lot from 20 January right up to 18 February. If you were born before the Chinese New Year, then you will belong to the previous year. For example, 19 January 1957 would count as 1956.

The next stage is to add together the last two numbers of your birth date: 5 + 6 = 11. If you arrive at a number higher than 9, then add these together: 1 + 1 = 2.

Now we get to the sexist bit. If you are female then add 5: 2 + 5 = 7. If you are male then this step is unnecessary due to some ancient idea about *yin* and *yang* which is a bit too complex to go into here. Remember that if the number you end up with is greater than 9, keep adding them together until you arrive at a single digit: your Star Number.

If you are male then you must now subtract your answer from 10 to arrive at your personal Star Number.

Elements and Directions

Each Star Number relates to an Element, and thus with one or more compass Directions (see box, opposite).

The reason that there are two lists for the number 5 is that this number is considered the most changeable of all, therefore it requires special attention for males and females.

Looking at the case studies opposite we can work out that because Julian was born on 14 September 1975, he is a 7 Metal person for whom a front door in a Westerly, North Westerly, South Westerly, Northern, or North Eastern Direction would be most fortunate (see box, below).

Julia, on the other hand, is an 8 Earth person so she would benefit from a front door which is aligned to the West, South, South West, North West or South East for maximum good fortune.

Of course, if you discover that your front door does not align with one of your fortunate Directions, turn to pages 25–26 for a few suggested remedies to improve your fortunes.

CASE STUDY

Julian was born on 14 September 1975. Since he wasn't born before the Chinese New Year, we add together the last two digits of his birth year: 7 + 5 = 12, and continue until we have a single number: 1 + 2 = 3. Because Julian is male, we now subtract this number from 10: 10 – 3 = 7. Therefore, Julian's personal Lucky Star Number is 7.

Julia was born on the same day so we again add together the last two digits of the birth year: 7 + 5 = 12, and continue as before: 1 + 2 = 3. Because Julia is female we now add 5: 3 + 5 = 8. Therefore, Julia's personal Lucky Star Number is 8.

YOUR STAR NUMBER, ELEMENT & DIRECTION

Star Number	Element	Harmonious Directions
1	Water	East, North, West, N. West, S. East
2	Earth	West, South, S. West, N. West, S. East
3	Wood	East, S. East, North, South
4	Wood	East, S. East, North, South
5 (for males)	Earth	West, South, S. West, N. West, S. East
5 (for females)	Earth	West, N. West, S. West, N. East
6	Metal	West, N. West, S. West, North, N. East
7	Metal	West, N. West, S. West, North, N. East
8	Earth	West, South, S. West, N. West, S. East
9	Fire	East, South, S. East, S. West, N.East

The Magic Square

Legend has it that the Magic Square, also known as the *Lo Shu,* originated from a remote period in China's history (estimated around 2205 BC) when the Emperor *Yu* apparently discovered it written on the back of a turtle. The Magic Square is probably the most ancient tool in use in the whole art of *feng-shui* and fortunately for us it is very easy to put into practice.

Basically the Magic Square is a 3 x 3 grid of small squares, each of which is allocated a number (those found on the back of the turtle). There are eight possible ways to add up the numbers, but they will always add up to 15 in whichever direction you choose.

The Magic Square is used in many ways, but we will only deal with one here. It is a grid map of the floor of your home which will tell you which sectors of your house relate to specific areas of your life. To accomplish this, draw out a rough map of the floor area of your home. If the floor area isn't exactly square don't worry, you simply elongate the Magic Square to fit, taking special note of any sector that falls outside

THE SQUARES & THEIR MEANINGS

4	9	2
3	5	7
8	1	6

Square 1 *(Front centre)*
Career prospects, your standing in your own eyes. Your potential in business dealings and the role you play in society.

Square 2 *(Rear right)*
Relationships of all kinds, especially romantic ones. Obviously marriage and long term partnerships are represented in this square.

Square 3 *(Middle left)*
The past, your ancestors and your original home are represented here. Family relationships through the generations and the prospects of inheritance.

Square 4 *(Rear left)*
This is the square that deals with prosperity. The prospects of gaining and keeping wealth are represented by this area.

Square 5 *(Centre)*
This square is very important because it is concerned with physical health and maintenance of well-being.

Square 6 *(Front right)*
In Chinese tradition this is the area of the gods and spirits. It represents those who would be willing to help you along. Friendly allies can be attracted by the proper use of this area.

Square 7 *(Middle right)*
This is the sector of children, fertility and creation. It may also manifest its energy as hobbies, creative gifts or even as a productive use of leisure time.

Square 8 *(Front left)*
This square relates to education and knowledge, and shows how open you are to new ideas. By extension it governs novelty coming into your life and how you react to it.

Square 9 *(Rear centre)*
The last square is the sector of fame. It governs your reputation, showing how you are viewed by others and the extent of the respect in which you are held.

your home. Now 'square it off', in other words, fill in the missing section on your map with a dotted line (see diagram, left).

Square by Square

Each numbered square has a precise significance in the life of the person living in that abode. The front door

THE EIGHT POINT METHOD

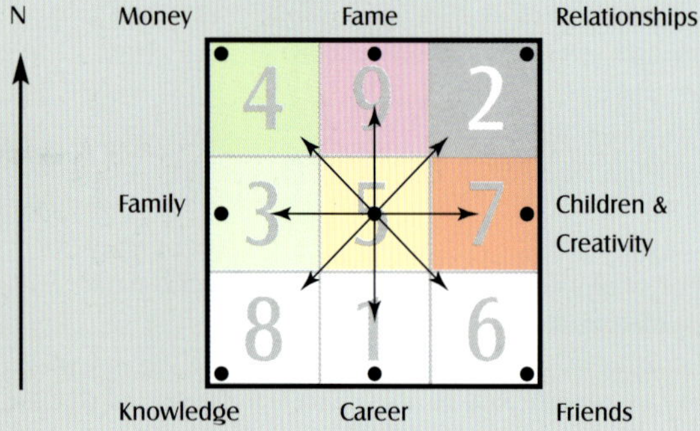

Stand in the centre of your house and divide your home into the remaining eight sectors of the Magic Square.

will be located in Squares 8, 1 or 6. It therefore follows that the centre of your home will occupy Square 5 and the furthest left-hand corner of your home will be in Square 4.

The Eight Point Method

If you are still unsure about the use of the Magic Square and the floor plan, try the Eight Point Method. This is so-called because you will be surrounded by eight significant areas when you stand at the centre of any given space in your home. First, stand in the middle of your home facing the direction of the front of the house or flat (to find the exact centre of your home simply draw diagonal lines from corner to corner on your squared off floor map (see diagram above). You are standing in Square 5, the area of health. To your left is Square 7, the area of children and creativity. To your right is Square 3, the sector of ancestors. Before you is Square 1, the Career sector and directly behind you is Square 9, the area of fame and reputation. The other squares will fill any gaps (see page 17 for their meanings).

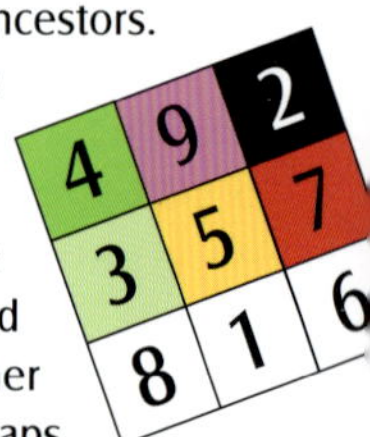

IRREGULAR DWELLINGS

If the Magic Square is not neatly contained within your walls because you live in an irregularly-shaped home, or it is in some other way incomplete then there will be a void area in your life. For example, an L-shaped dwelling could have one or two sectors missing and this could damage the potentials of your fortune. Problems can also occur when one or more areas are enlarged. Many houses have extensions which will unbalance the *feng-shui* of the building. In either case, the method of balancing the rest of the home by use of colour or symbols is important. There are several ways of bringing your home into a harmonious state, which will be explained throughout this book.

It is rare that anyone lives in a home which is perfectly square or rectangular. Equally, many flats and apartments are extremely irregular in shape, effectively 'cutting out' various points of the Magic Square. If this is the case then it may be an idea to deal with each room individually, by dividing each into its own Magic Square.

FENG SHUI REMEDIES

Cure 1: *If one of your Eight Points is missing then add mirrors to one or more walls as required to provide an illusion of more space. The best place for a mirror is at the point where the diagonal line meets the wall (see above).*

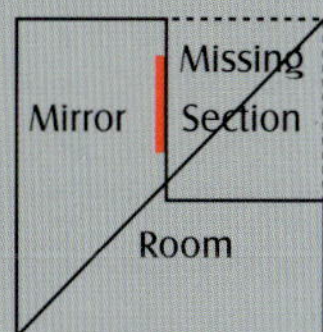

Cure 2: *If one of your Eight Points is elongated or exaggerated in some way, check the Direction of that sector and take note of the Element that governs it. Refer to pages 12–13 for the remedy.*

Putting it All Together

It is at this point that *feng-shui* starts to get really interesting. We have seen how you have a personal Star Number, are ruled by a particular Element and have a set of lucky and unlucky Directions. Now we'll begin by putting these factors together to assess your personal fortune and that of your home.

First of all draw a floor map of your home as accurately as you possibly can. Draw in the doors, walls and the positions of the windows. If your home is of an irregular shape, such as an L-shape, then fill in the missing part with a dotted line to square it off.

Look at the Magic Square diagrams on pages 16–18 and imagine that this is the floor plan of your home. Now draw light lines from corner to corner to find the exact centre of your home. This is the Health Area which corresponds to sector 5 in the Magic Square diagram. Incidentally, this is a good place to hang a wind-chime to generate beneficial *chi.*

The front door (or the door which you habitually use) will be situated in one of the bottom three sectors of the Magic Square: 1, 8 or 6. Therefore the luck that enters your home will tend to influence your career, your education or arrive via your friends.

To check, stand in the centre of your home facing the front of the house or flat (the wall that the main door is in). You will now be able to mentally divide your home into the various sectors of the Magic Square. If you stand in the area of health, the sector of fame will be directly behind you, and the career square in front. To your left will be the sector of children and creativity and to your right will be family and heritage. The money area is over your right shoulder, the sector of relationships over your left. Diagonally to your left

CASE STUDY

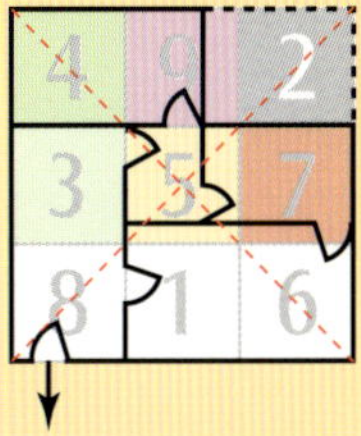

Front Door South

Remember Julian and Julia, our examples from page 15? We have already worked out that Julian's personal Star Number is 7 and that Julia's Star Number is 8. This means that Julian is governed by the Metal Element, while Julia is ruled by the Earth Element. Thus, the best Direction for Julian's front door is North, North West, South West, West and North East. Unfortunately, as luck would have it, his front door faces towards the South (see diagram, above) which is an unfortunate Direction for him. The remedy for this is simple, he should paint the door either white, the colour of the Metal Element (his own ruling Element) or dark blue or black the colour of the Water Element (which is compatible to him).

Potential troubles are also possible in his other favourable Directions: the North West, North East, West and South West (see problem areas and colour cures for a south-facing front door on page 26). If Julian stands in the centre of his home he can work out the sectors of the Magic Square for these Directions by the Eight Point Method (see page 18).

Because the area of self knowledge (Direction South West, Square 8) is afflicted, he may be confused about his aims while he lives in this home. The remedy for this is to paint this room white (see page 26) or add items that are metallic.

Home and heritage (Direction West, Square 3) too will bring him problems concerning his parents if he doesn't bring some Earth Element into this area. He could do this by decorating it yellow (see page 26), or by adding a stone, a square rug or a picture of an emperor, the symbolic feature of Earth (see page 12).

The same problems may also occur in the North West Direction which is his money area. This too relates to Earth and the same remedies apply.

The last problem sector is the North East which rules relationships. The Element Metal must be prominent, so he could decorate the area white (see page 26), add metal objects or a sculpture of a tiger (the symbolic animal of Metal, see page 12).

These remedies, plus a wind-chime in the centre of the home should improve Julian's life no end.

Sharp corners, junctions and aerials create 'secret arrows'.

is the sector of friends and diagonally right is the sector of education and self knowledge.

Secret Arrows

When you look out from your main door, check for 'secret arrow' makers, such as sharp corners, telegraph poles, satellite dishes and the like, which point in the direction of the door. If these are present (and these days it is difficult to get away from them), fasten the *Pa Kua* mirror supplied with this book to the door, or just inside the door if it is partially made of glass (failing that placing it in a front window will work just as well). Make sure that you've got the mirror the right way up: the three unbroken lines should be at the top.

CASE STUDY

Plants and soft furnishings enliven the Northern sector.

Julia's front door faces West which is one of her fortunate Directions so she need not change the colour or anything else about her front door. A lamp-post directly outside her door, however, could send 'secret arrows' shooting her way so the positioning of a *Pa Kua* mirror would be beneficial.

Because her door is facing a Westerly Direction her problem areas will be North, South, South East and East (see page 26). These relate to heritage and ancestors (North), children and creativity (South), relationships (South East) and reputation (East).

Her relationship with her parents can be improved by the addition of the Element Wood in the Northern sector. Therefore, it should be decorated in green or have wooden objects, healthy plants and possibly the image of a dragon in it.

Her chances of netting a mate (governed by the South East) will be improved by placing an emphasis on the Water Element in the South East. Therefore this area should be decorated in dark blue or black, with the addition of a fish tank or a statue of a tortoise, both of which symbolize Water. The same applies to her reputation (East).

If Julia wants children or to ensure the success of creative projects then an emphasis on the Earth Element in the Southern sector (painting it yellow, a square rug, placing stones there) will give her a greater chance of achieving her objectives. Now try this method out on your own home.

The Front Door, Hallway & Stairs

The front door is the most important *feng-shui* influence in the home. After all, it is through it that your luck arrives, whether in the form of visitors or of mail. Many homes use a side or back door as the main means of access, so if that is the case, then the Direction of that door is important.

In oriental tradition the front door is considered the 'mouth' of the house through which the sustenance of the home is taken. It can also be the most vulnerable point if 'secret arrows', which bring disorder and bad luck, are found.

The Direction the front door faces is very important. It should align with one of your lucky Directions according to your personal Star Number, but on no account should it face one of those Directions from which misfortune can come (see box, below). This factor is

YOUR BEST FRONT DOOR DIRECTION

Star Number	Best Direction	Next Best	Worst
1	South East	North	North West
2	North East	South West	South
3	South	East	North East
4	North	South East	West
5 (for a man)	North East	South West	South
5 (for a woman)	South West	North East	East
6	West	North West	North
7	North West	West	South East
8	South West	North East	East
9	East	South	South West

FENG-SHUI REMEDIES FOR THE FRONT DOOR

Cure 1: *If your front door has 'secret arrows' directed at it or it faces a negative area, such as a T-junction, the use of the* Pa Kua *mirror (supplied with this book) is strongly recommended. Hang the mirror outside the door (facing away from the house) to deflect ill fortune. If this is not practical, hang it in a glass panel inside the door or in a front window (always facing outwards). If this remedy does not appeal, you may consider a large brassy, reflective door-knob to bounce back the negative* sha. *Remember to keep it well polished.*

Cure 2: *If your front door faces a negative Direction you may consider re-painting it a more auspicious colour – one that is more in tune with the Element that relates to your Star Number.*

Cure 3: *Symbolic images can be placed in or near the doorway. A wind-chime can improve* chi, *or the placement of a bamboo flute just within the door will help to dispel harmful energies. You might even consider placing a picture of a tiger (always facing towards the entrance) in the hall, especially if the door faces West or you were born under the Metal Element (see page 12).*

Cure 4: *If nothing seems to work to improve your luck, then drastic action is required. Block the offending front door off and use another door as your main entrance, if possible.*

equally true if you live in an apartment, but there is an added complication because you will deal with the door of your home, and that of the building separately.

Classical Chinese tradition states that a curving path should lead to the door, a pond should lie to one side of this path and your property should be protected by a low wall. However, none of these criteria are strictly necessary, which is a good thing since so many of us live off a terraced street or a hallway.

The Front Door

Firstly let's look at your Star Number. If you haven't worked out your Star Number yet, see pages 14–15. Then look at the table opposite to work out your best and worst front door Directions. The list of Directions for

PROBLEM AREAS AND COLOUR CURES

Each of these boxes shows the potential problem areas (coloured sectors) for a house with a front door facing each of the eight compass Directions. Painting the rooms of the house that are situated in the problem areas the colour suggested for that Direction will help to remedy potential bad luck in the afflicted area.

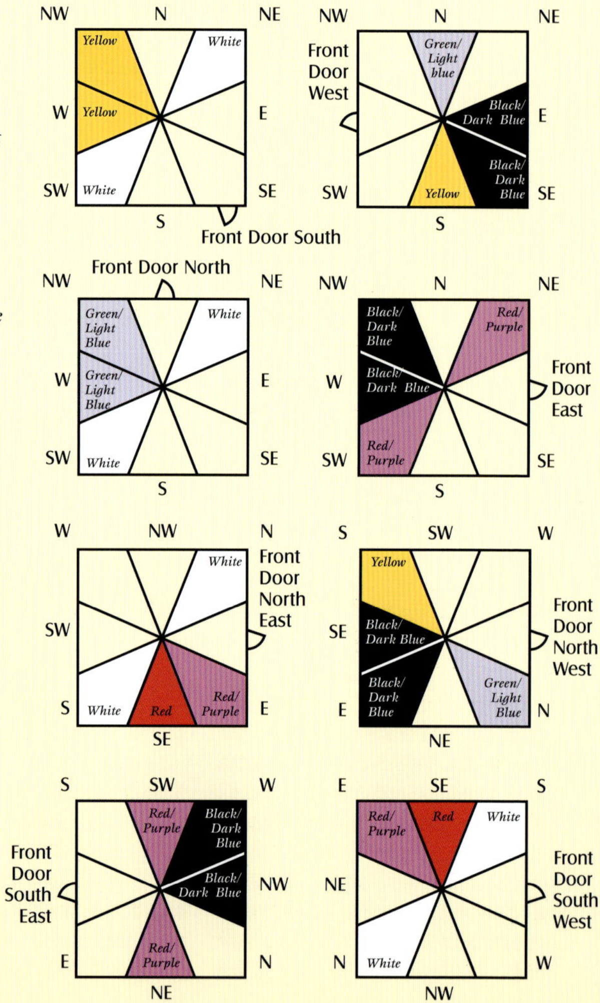

Since sha *travels in straight lines, a curving path leading to your door will promote prosperity and good fortune.*

The Back Door

This door is not as important as the front door of your dwelling (unless of course, you use it as the main method of access in which case treat the back door as the front door and vice versa). However, this secondary door does symbolize indirect opportunities: chances which occur to others yet by which you will benefit.

Although glass in the front door is frowned upon in feng-shui, *it is positively encouraged in the back door. An expanse of glass here will encourage* chi *into your home.*

An open area behind your house will promote peace and harmony in your abode. Obstructions just outside the door, however, will obstruct the free flow of chi *so they should be removed immediately.*

your Star Number (see page 15) are also considered important for your front door. These Directions should be an important consideration when you are choosing a new place to live. After all, a prospective home may seem ideal, but if it it is fated to bring misery and bad luck, you should think again.

The basic rules are that the main door should not face any obstacle, such as a high wall or fence. It should not face a T-junction, the end of a bridge or the outer edge of a sharp bend in the road (remember that *sha chi*, or bad energy, travels in straight lines). However, even if your front door does fall into one of these catagories, all is not lost (see remedies, pages 25–26).

Ideally, there should be a winding path leading to the entrance, as this will increase the wealth of the home. Now stand at your door looking outwards. Take note of any telegraph poles, lamp-posts or corners pointing towards you. A satellite dish pointing directly at the door is the most modern 'secret arrow' maker. This will cause negative energy which, if ignored, can disrupt the harmony of your home.

The front door itself should be of solid construction, symbolizing protection. Therefore, although glass is generally encouraged in *feng-shui,* its use in the front door should be limited.

The Hallway

The front door should not open into a narrow or constricted hallway because this will limit the free movement of *chi* and restrict the potential of any good luck entering your home. It is important that the hall should be light and airy, even if it is a narrow corridor. A row of small mirrors positioned at head height along one wall of the corridor should help the flow of *chi,* especially if they reflect an attractive picture placed on the opposite wall.

The first thing one sees when entering the house is said to have a profound influence on the inhabitants. Therefore something attractive, such as a decorative urn, a plant or beautiful painting, will increase good fortune, while a plain and rather shoddy hallway will fritter away *chi* almost before it has arrived.

FENG SHUI REMEDIES FOR THE HALLWAY AND STAIRS

Cure 1: *If your hallway is dark and constricted, redecoration in a lighter more positive shade is recommended. The addition of colourful pictures and a row of mirrors placed at head height will improve the flow of* chi.

Cure 2: *If the stairway directly aligns with the front door a long rug with lots of curves in the pattern will retard the swift flow of* chi *and allow it to circulate more freely. You may even wish to consider adding an inner door to add a barrier between the stairs and the entrance.*

The Stairway

Although *feng-shui* tradition frowns on a stairway directly in line with the front door, in many Western houses this is a standard feature. Ideally, the stairs should not align with the front door at the end of a long straight hall (remember *sha chi* travels in straight lines), but should gently curve to increase the flow of *chi.* If your stairs are in line with the passageway and front door, see the box on the left for effective remedies.

In addition, the positioning of a mirror at the foot of the stairs is thought to be a bad mistake as it is considered to promote accidents.

Curved stairs increase the flow of good *chi* into the home.
The hallway should be light and well-ventilated to encourage *chi* to enter the home.
Beautiful objects, such as paintings, will increase good fortune.
If the stairs are directly in line with the front door, place a rug with a curvy pattern depicted on it on the floor in front of the stairs so that the *chi* is encouraged to flow gently around the room.

The Living Room

The living room is the very heart of the house. It is the area in which most time is spent and consequently should be comfortable and promote peace and relaxation. It is also the room in which most entertaining is done, therefore it should be welcoming and aesthetically pleasing. This last point is particularly important since the decoration of this room should express something about your own personality as well as providing space for your personal possessions, such as a sofa, chairs, TV and hi-fi.

The Eight Point Method (see page 18) comes into its own when examining the living room. The living room should be analyzed separately from the rest of the home and the furnishings placed accordingly. Firstly, stand in the doorway facing into the living room. The corner furthest to your right is the 'power corner', which is also the area of relationships. This is the best place to site your TV or hi-fi, especially if you place a memento of a loved one there, too. A photograph of your lover or partner on the TV or a treasured gift from your beloved would be a good solution.

Apart from the 'power corner', the money and friendship sectors are also very important in relation to the living room.

Positive Factors

The living room should be welcoming. It should be a happy place in which you are pleased to spend time and entertain friends and family. The *yang* nature of this room,

BAD FENG-SHUI IN THE LIVING ROOM

This illustration shows a very uncomfortable lounge area. The two chairs are so badly placed that stressful thoughts can be expected if too much time is spent there. The TV in the 'Friends' sector would promote unrealistic expectations while the cluttered coffee table in the centre would adversely affect health. In addition, the TV should not stand directly in front of a window becasue this will cause glare which feng-shui *masters regard as a form of* sha chi.

whether you have decorated it in a formal or casual style, will affect your relationships and success. Because the living room is strongly *yang*, you should add some *yin* touches to soften its masculine energies. Some scatter cushions, soft furnishings, leafy, green, healthy plants, and possibly a goldfish tank will ensure a pleasant atmosphere.

Remedies for Negative Factors

The centre of the living room should be left uncluttered. If, however, your coffee table is positioned in the middle of the room, ensure that it is never constantly covered in dirty dishes, mugs or newspapers. Remember that the centre of the living room represents the health area and the last thing you want is to cause complications here. A rectangular living room calls for a rectangular coffee table. If the room is square then a round or octagonal table would be a good feature.

Chairs should not be positioned with their backs to the main door as this will transfer negative *sha* into the adjoining room. In addition, your favourite chair should not have its back to a window or be placed under a heavy beam as both of these factors will create anxiety and stress.

Another negative factor to watch out for concerns the fireplace. Although fire creates *chi,* a chimney will draw *chi* from the room. Therefore, if the fireplace is in a good Direction in relation to the main door of the home and doesn't fall in a problem area (see page 26), it is a good idea to place a mirror above the fireplace as this will reflect *chi* back into the room rather than it being sucked up the chimney. If the Direction of the fireplace is not in one of the good areas then do not hang a mirror above it because the *chi* will escape. On the subject of fireplaces, a fire-guard is always a good idea and will help to prevent *chi* from being lost up the chimney.

Generally speaking, the main door to the living room should not directly face the window or another door as the *chi* will swiftly dissipate from the room. If your lounge is so afflicted, place a screen between the opposing factors or put up a blind or net curtains at the window to solve the problem.

Arranging your Living Room

Fortunately, arranging a living room to *feng-shui* perfection is not difficult if you follow some simple rules. One of the functions of a relaxed living area is to promote communication and better understanding between people. Therefore, conversation is considered to be very important. To encourage this interchange of views, face two chairs or sofas at a slight angle towards each other across the room. Having seating arrangements directly facing each other may be regarded as being confrontational. The 'horseshoe' shape is said to be the most favourable arrangement of furniture, as long as the chairs or sofa do not back on to the doorway.

Wherever possible, furniture should be positioned against the walls. Failing that, furniture should at least be placed parallel to a wall. Try to avoid placing a chair or sofa in front of a door or window as this will make the occupant feel very vulnerable.

If you have opposing doors in your living room, try to avoid placing one chair on one side of the openings, while the others face it from the other side. This could have the effect of isolating a family member and ultimately lead to frayed tempers.

Don't place chairs underneath exposed beams because the sitter will feel oppressed. If this can't be avoided hang something suggestive of airiness on the beam. The traditional Chinese cure is to hang a pair of bamboo flutes here.

When placing your favourite chair, traditional *feng-shui* principles state that it is favourable to have your back

SEATING ARRANGEMENTS IN THE LIVING ROOM

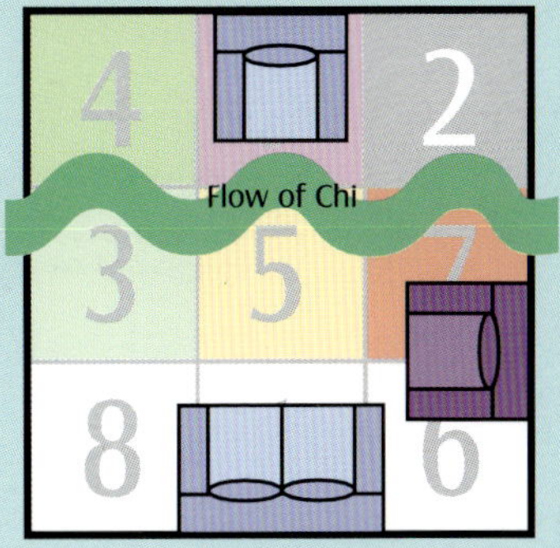

The positioning of the furniture in the diagram on the left will create alienation, loneliness and frayed tempers. The unfavourable arrangement means that chi, *and therefore good energy, is not allowed to circulate around the room and thus does not benefit the occupants.*

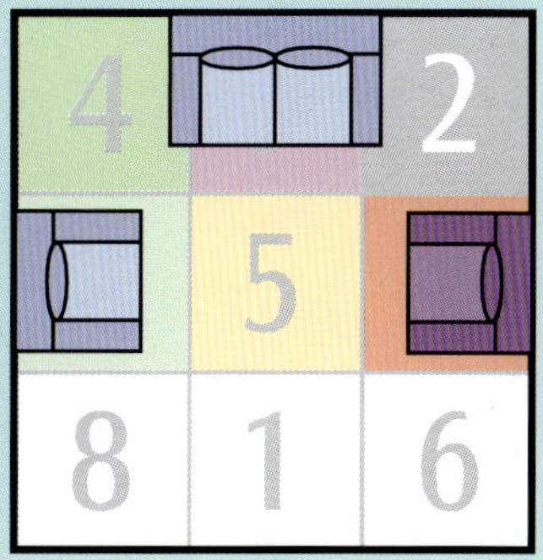

The positioning of the furniture in the diagram on the right forms a 'horseshoe' shape which allows chi *to circulate and thus encourages conversation and communication.*

to your luckiest Directions (see page 15) as this will encourage beneficial energy to enter your physical body.

Your furniture should be in tune with the size and shape of the room. If your furniture is oversized and makes the room feel cramped, you will find that a similar 'cramping' will occur in your life, reducing your options in many spheres of activity. Likewise if the furniture is too small, uncomfortable or in some other way unsuitable for the space, you will start to feel a certain deficiency in your life.

One final point, a Southerly facing living room is suitable for those who wish to rise early and love the healthy lifestyle. A Westerly facing living room is more in tune with those who like to talk and laugh long into the night.

FENG-SHUI REMEDIES

Cure 1: *The addition of healthy, bright and vibrant plants will encourage* chi *and can help to soften 'secret arrows'. Dried flowers are a bad idea, as they symbolize death.*

Cure 2: *The placement of a mirror above the fireplace will encourage* sha chi *to be sucked up the chimney.*

Cure 3: *As the living room is* yang *in nature, add some soft furnishings, such as scatter cushions, to add a touch of* yin.

A light and airy room is excellent *feng-shui.*

An uncluttered coffee table in the middle of the room is good *feng-shui.*

Curved windows promote the flow of *chi.*
The urn provides a protective barrier against the loss of *chi* up the chimney.
The horseshoe shape is the most favourable arrangement for furniture.

The Dining Room

The Chinese believe that the process of eating provides nourishment for both the body and the spirit, so any distraction during a meal will cause *sha chi*. This means that eating your food on a tray on your knees while watching TV is bad *feng-shui*.

If at all possible use one room specifically for the consumption of food. Failing that a distinct area of the living room or kitchen should be set aside for the purpose. You may wish to use plants and screens to block off the eating area so that you aren't distracted by the rest of your environment.

It is not a good idea to position the dining area too near to the main door of your home because according to *feng-shui* tradition this will promote gluttony and a lack of hospitality.

The focus of the dining area should be the table and its contents so it is not a good idea to decorate this room or area with busy patterns. Nothing should distract you from the fact that you are eating a meal.

The table should be the central feature of this space. Chinese tradition suggests that it should be circular or octagonal in shape rather than square or rectangular. The reason for this is that sharp corners generate 'secret arrows' and these may cause digestive problems and an irritable mood amongst your guests.

Chairs should be even in number because even numbers represent good fortune while odd numbers symbolize loneliness. The addition of an extra chair, even if it does not match the others, is preferable to an odd number.

Ideally, dining chairs should be comfortable so that the diner will take time to eat. If the chairs have arms it will encourage good luck and help communication during meals.

Avoid placing dining chairs with their backs to doors or windows.
A circular or octagonal dining table is convivial to good conversation.
Curved armed chairs promote comfort and relaxation which are important factors in a good meal.

The Kitchen

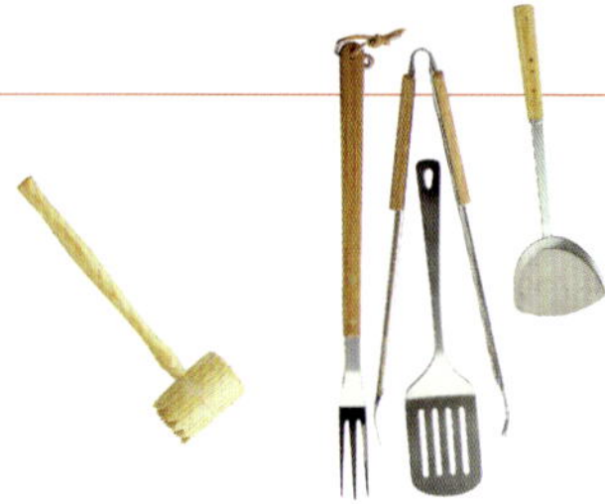

The kitchen is seen to be the 'stomach' of the house and is therefore associated with the nourishment and health of the family. *Feng-shui* tradition states that if the kitchen is mis-aligned or the oven, sink and refrigerator are in inappropriate positions, financial loss and health problems can occur.

The kitchen door should be large enough to allow the free flow of *chi* throughout the room. Ideally, it should not be directly aligned with the front door of the house, or in line with a window or internal door as this will cause *chi* to flow through the kitchen too quickly and not allow any benefits to accrue.

In general *feng-shui* terms, the kitchen should not be contained in the North, North East or North West sectors of a home because ancient sages considered these Watery Directions incompatible with the fiery nature of cooking.

Commonsense dictates that the kitchen should be clean, well-lit and adequately ventilated. It should not be positioned next to a bathroom because the uses of the two rooms are incompatible. However, in many house plans, the bathroom does indeed share a wall with the kitchen, so in this case there shouldn't be a direct access from one room to the other. The general rule about unnecessary clutter should also be observed in the kitchen.

The Oven

The single most important feature in any kitchen is the oven, the place where food is cooked. The oven is ruled by the Fire Element and the Direction it faces is of paramount importance. It should not face either the front or back doors because this is considered to be very bad luck. Preventing this from occurring also means that the cook does not have his or her back to the door. If, however, you cannot avoid this happening, hang a small mirror above the stove so that the cook is aware of what is going on behind him or her. The oven should not be positioned directly under a skylight or window as this will tend to dissipate good fortune.

Feng-shui tradition states that there is a favourable Direction for the oven which is called *T'ien yi.* This varies from person to person but it relates to your 'Star Number' (see page 15).

It is a good idea to keep your stove top clean. This is not only hygienic but it ensures that your income will remain steady. Also, remember to use all of the burners or hot plates on the stove to ensure that the energy flows evenly and your money luck increases.

Fire and Water

The oven is associated with the Fire Element, so it is important that it does not directly face the sink or the refrigerator, both of which are ruled by the Water Element. If they are in opposition, there are a couple of easy remedies to improve the *feng-shui.*

The colour green should be an important feature in a kitchen because it symbolizes the Element Wood which balances the Fire and Water Elements of the appliances as shown in the Creative Cycle, see pages 10–13.

If, however the sink or refrigerator are situated alongside the oven, then the addition of the Element Wood in the area between them will harmonize these energies – try a plant or a wooden ornament. The more practically minded may prefer to add a wooden bread-board, storage unit or wooden cooking utensils in this area.

THE BEST AND WORST DIRECTIONS FOR YOUR OVEN

Star Number	Best Direction for Oven	Worst Directions
1	East	North West
2	West	South
3	North	North East
4	South	West
5 (for a man)	West	South
5 (for a woman)	North West	East
6	North East	North & South
7	South West	South East
8	North West	East
9	South East	South West

FENG-SHUI REMEDIES

Cure 1: *Hang a green tea-towel over the handle of the oven door, or in front of the sink.*

Cure 2: *Place green flooring or a green rug between the oven and the sink.*

The kitchen symbolizes the family's wealth, health and happiness. Overall, the kitchen should be clean, clutter-free, well-lit and adequately ventilated in order to aid the feng-shui of the house and its occupants to the very best advantage.

Good light is very important in a kitchen as it promotes positive energy.

The round edges of this table allow the positive energy of *chi* to circulate freely.

Jutting corner cupboards and sharp, pointed shelves can cause unhappiness and ill-health.

The position of the oven is very important. It should not face the sink or refrigerator because the Element of Water clashes with the Element of Fire.

The cook should not be in such a position that his or her back is facing towards the kitchen door.

The Bedroom

The most important feature of the bedroom is, of course, the bed. And since we spend at least a third of our lives asleep, its position and Direction is considered vital in *feng-shui* terms. Many of the *feng-shui* principles relating to the bedroom are designed to promote a sense of well-being and harmony that will ensure complete rest and reduce any neuroses or unease.

The *feng-shui* rules for the sleeping area are more of a list of 'don'ts' rather than a list of 'do's'. This is because the nature of the bedroom is *yin,* or passive, rather than one in which active living is done.

Feng-shui Advice

There are several rules about the position of the bed that really must not be broken. For example, the bedroom should only have one entrance so that the good *chi* may enter and circulate around the room rather than rapidly passing through from door to door. Most importantly you should not sleep with your head pointed towards the doorway. This is commonsense because if you are unable to see anyone entering the room from this position, you will always feel ill at ease. Equally, your feet should not point directly at the door. This is thought to be because this is the way coffins were carried out when someone died.

If you have an en-suite bathroom your feet should not point towards the door either because this Water-ruled room will draw physical energy away from you. The same applies to windows, but in this case neither your head nor your feet should point directly at a window.

Exposed beams create feelings of anxiety and disturb sleep patterns.
Dried flowers promote illness.
Metal bedsteads, electric blankets and pictures above the bed create a sense of threat from 'secret arrows' and too much *sha.*
Healthy plants are always a good idea as they encourage *chi.*
Try to avoid angular furniture as it causes 'secret arrows'. Rounded furniture is preferred as it encourages *chi.*

Ideally, the bedroom should not be positioned above an unoccupied space, a garage or storeroom because any positive energy in the bedroom will be drawn through the floor and may cause bad luck to the sleeper.

A sloping ceiling in the bedroom is also bad *feng-shui* because the oppressive nature of the ceiling will act on the unconscious mind of the sleeper and cause anxieties and depression. An overhead beam positioned directly above the bed is even worse and may cause bad dreams as well. The same applies to pictures above the bed-head or a chandelier hanging directly above the bed – they are a threat to a good night's sleep.

Electricity, which is strongly Yang, should have a limited presence in the bedroom. Therefore, TV sets, videos and other electronic equipment should be somehow obscured from view when not in use. A screen of some kind would be a good idea.

Electric blankets are definitely frowned upon in *feng-shui* teaching. If you really must use one then make sure that it is the type that can be turned off before you retire.

Provided your bedroom is large enough, wardrobes can be placed diagonally across corners to round off and soften the angular outlines of the bedroom.

Mirrors in the Bedroom

Whereas *feng-shui* teachings in general encourage the use of mirrors to remedy certain problems, mirrors are not looked upon favourably in the bedroom. In fact, mirrors are not encouraged except at the foot of the bed. Ideally, if mirrors are present (and what bedroom doesn't have at least one?), they should be covered before retiring. Failing that they should be kept out of the eye-line of the sleeper. This is because the Chinese believe that the soul leaves the body during sleep and it may be frightened by its own reflection in the mirror on returning. The fleeing soul would then depart forever with apparently fatal consequences.

The Bed

It should be possible to get into bed from either side, unless, that is, you wish to sleep alone. The recommended distance of the bed to the nearest wall should not be less than 60 cm/ 2 ft.

Bedsteads made of metal can shoot 'secret arrows' at the sleeper and care must be taken that the corners of angular furniture do not point in the sleeper's direction for they too will create 'secret arrows'. If your bedstead is made of brass or iron then wrap the exposed metal in fabric to soften the harsh outline.

LUCKY DIRECTIONS FOR THE BED

Just as in other important places in the home, the establishment of the lucky Direction for the head of the bed is very important. This Direction is called *Nien Yen* which means longevity of descendants and is a considerable help to relationship happiness. You will again need your Star Number so refresh your memory by glancing back at pages 14–15.

I should point out that it is unlikely that you will have a convenient wall in just the right Direction, and since the head of the bed should be against a wall it would be better to follow this rule rather than moving your bed to the centre of the room.

However, if you do align your bed towards your lucky Direction and by doing so you break one of the unbreakable rules, such as making the foot of the bed face a door or window or placing yourself under a central beam, then it would be best to ignore the whole thing. It is much more important to achieve a good night's sleep than increase your luck here since that can be made up for elsewhere in the house.

On the other hand, the lucky Directions for the bed become more important if you are trying to conceive a child since these are traditionally said to increase fertility.

THE BEST DIRECTION FOR THE BED

Star Number	Best Direction for Headboard
1	South
2	North West
3	South East
4	East
5 for a man	North West
5 for a woman	West
6	South West
7	North East
8	West
9	North

Similarly, rounded furniture is preferable in the bedroom, but you can drape fabric over angular furniture to soften it. Make sure that you have plenty of scatter cushions to promote softness and comfort.

Four-poster beds aren't good *feng-shui,* but their negative effect can be minimized by covering straight columns. If you have a four-poster bed with spiral columns then much of the negative *sha* is dissipated.

A Child's Bedroom

The bedroom of a child or infant is regarded somewhat differently to other bedrooms in *feng-shui.* Ideally, it should be in the South Eastern sector of your home if you live North of the equator, or in the North Eastern sector if you live South of the equator. The main reason behind this is to ensure that the life-giving *yang* energy of the rising sun will benefit the health of a child with abundant *chi.*

It is considered favourable if a child's bedroom is rectangular in shape, with natural light and good ventilation, and in close proximity to the parent's bedroom. If the room is naturally dark, then a mobile or wind-chime should be hung outside the window, or if this is not possible, just within the window.

The window of a child's bedroom should look out on to life. *Feng-shui* tradition states that a view of a garden, shrubbery and healthy plants is vital, but a busy street is also buzzing with life and would be beneficial (however, if it is too busy there may be a problem with noise). In any case, a touch of greenery on the windowsill will create the necessary *chi* in the room.

Light green should be a prominent colour in a child's bedroom because this relates to the Element Wood and suggests the sprouting growth of young plants as well as the Easterly direction, suggestive of the rising sun.

Soft, organic furnishing, too, should be included – woollen carpets, wood panelling or wallpaper are all associated with the Element Wood and growth.

If the child is a boy then he will be *yang* in nature, therefore the addition

Wooden furniture is good for a child's bedroom as it encourages health and growth.

of *yin* blues and cool colours will add balance to his character. The opposite is true of girls who are basically *yin*, some warm *yang* tones will encourage self-confidence.

The rules for the placement of the child's bed are as for the main bedroom (see pages 42–45). It should not face the door or window, but should have a wall at its head and along one side.

The Bathroom & Toilet

Running water is a vital component of the art of *feng-shui* and this aspect comes into its own when considering the bathroom and toilet. The location of this room is generally pretty fixed and not usually a matter of choice, therefore it is a relief to find that its position within the home is not too crucial.

Feng-shui does, however, frown on a toilet positioned immediately next to the front door, in the centre of the house or adjacent to a kitchen. However, if your toilet is situated in one of these areas, there are *feng-shui* cures that will help to remedy the situation (see opposite). Generally, you will need lots more *yang,* masculine, positive energy in your home to offset the negative forces of the toilet which can manifest as health problems, no matter how hygienic you are.

The toilet and bathroom are basically *yin,* or passive, in nature as they fall under the rulership of the Element Water. The toilet is one of those areas which cannot benefit from the flow of *chi,* and if certain precautions are not taken, *sha chi* or dead energy can be generated which can negatively affect the health of the occupants.

The toilet itself is a danger point since by its very function it flushes away unwanted matter and if you aren't careful it can flush away your prosperity, marital happiness and peace of mind just as easily.

The basic rules of siting the toilet according to *feng-shui* principles would satisfy any building inspector or sanitary engineer. For example, the toilet should not directly face the front door and, if possible, there should be a ventilated lobby between the toilet and the rest of the home. In addition, if at all possible, the toilet should not be located next to the kitchen or open directly off the living area.

The worst possible Directions for a toilet to face are considered to be the best ones for your front door. However, even if your toilet does face your worst Direction, remember there are remedies to prevent your wealth from being flushed away (see below). Fortunately, there are more options for the Direction the toilet faces than for any other feature of the house.

DIRECTIONS FOR YOUR BATHROOM AND TOILET

Star Number	Worst Toilet Direction	Best Toilet Directions
1	South East	South West, North West, North East
2	North East	North, South East, South
3	South	West, North West, North East
4	North	South West, West, North East
5 (for a man)	North East	North, South East, South
5 (for a woman)	South West	North, East, South East
6	West	North, East, South
7	North West	East, South East, South
8	South West	North, East, South East
9	East	South West, West, North West

FENG-SHUI REMEDIES FOR THE TOILET

Cure 1: *If your toilet faces an unfavourable Direction for you, there is a remedy that doesn't require demolishing your bathroom! The answer is deceptively simple: ensure that the toilet door is shut and keep the toilet lid down (especially when flushing). If this proves insufficient then consider a full length mirror placed on the outside of the toilet door and also position four opposing mirrors within the bathroom itself.*

Cure 2: *A wooden toilet seat and wooden bathroom fittings are very good* feng-shui. *The Element Wood is generated from the Element Water so good fortune can be expected from such an auspicious arrangement.*

Cure 3: *If you feel as if your resources are draining away, place a small mirror facing the toilet. If this means positioning it on the inside of the door so much the better because it will prevent more cash draining away. If this remedy is not practical then stick a small mirror to the base of the toilet to dispel* sha chi.

FENG-SHUI REMEDIES FOR THE BATHROOM

Cure 1: *Make sure that all taps and cisterns are functioning correctly. A dripping tap or leaky cistern can drain away your money as fast as it comes in. Another effect could be that some of your friends may become a constant drain on your resources. So to ensure that your friends are genuine and have your best interests at heart, get the plumber in!*

Cure 2: *Many modern houses include a bathroom without a window. This is very bad in* feng-shui *terms. If you are the unfortunate possessor of such a room then surround the walls with mirrors, the bigger the better. Ideally, there should be at least four mirrors in the bathroom, each one facing its opposite. However, if this isn't possible then two mirrors will do as long as they face each other. The mirrors will create a swirling motion of beneficial* chi *and, strangely enough, we are told it dispels lingering odours!*

Cure 3: *Healthy potted plants would be a good feature if your bathroom has a window. Plants relate to the Element Wood so they are elementally compatible too.*

Two mirrors facing each other encourage good *chi* to circulate in a windowless bathroom.

Cure 4: *Some candles would add much needed* yang *to this most* yin *of rooms.*

Cure 5: *If you have a ventilation device in the bathroom, then hanging some brightly coloured ribbons or a wind-chime will replace lost* chi *when the device is turned on.*

It is thought that venetian blinds create 'secret
Healthy trailing plants will help to soften sharp corners that create 'secret arrows'.
Dried flowers should be avoided as they add extra *yin* to this most *yin* of rooms.
The bathroom is ruled by the Water Element so wooden fittings are very good *feng-shui.*

The Home Office

Although work activities can take place anywhere in the home, it would be better if the home office was situated in one of your fortunate areas according to your Star Number (see pages 14–15), or in the Money, Career or Creative sectors of the Magic Square (see page 18).

The study or home office should combine a calm environment conducive to concentration with an atmosphere that is mentally alert. For example, cool *yin* shades will focus the mind, and soft lighting will help to calm the spirit.

The Magic Square has great relevance to your desk or table-top, too. It, like the floor area of your home, can be divided into the nine areas of the Magic Square to ensure prosperity and success.

The Office and the Bedroom

If your workspace is in a bedroom there should be a clear division of space so that the work station does not spill over into the sleeping area. A barrier, such as a book case, would work well to separate psychologically the incompatible functions of the room. You may have to use considerable ingenuity to get the *feng-shui* just right. The secret of making this arrangement viable is to leave the room at intervals during the working day to do something else so that you associate the area with being two separate spaces instead of one. For example, a computer in a bedroom/office should be covered at night to prevent the screen from acting as a mirror and causing restlessness.

A good mental attitude is going to be essential if you combine a work area with a sleeping area. Don't go directly from bed to desk or vice versa. For example, on waking, leave the room, make yourself a drink and then return to do some work.

The Desk

The placement of the desk within your work-room is of prime importance. It is bad *feng-shui* to position a desk directly facing a window because glare will tend to strain the eyes. Likewise it is not a good idea to place a desk with its back to a window as this will create a subconscious feeling of unease.

The desk should face in the general direction of the door. It doesn't have to be precise but it is important that you do not have your back to the door, otherwise you will never be master within your own home or business. However if it is impossible to align your desk or working area without breaking these rules you can always screen off the offending window or door. If you don't possess a folding screen, a few well-placed healthy plants will work just as well. With the rules about the window and door in mind we should now find out the most auspicious Direction for the desk (see box, above right).

Remembering that clutter and piles of paper should be avoided wherever possible, clear your desk top to create a harmonious environment. Imagine the nine segments of the Magic

BEST DESK POSITION

Star Number	Best Desk Direction
1	South East
2	North East
3	South
4	North
5 (for males)	North East
5 (for females)	South West
6	West
7	North West
8	South West
9	East

The diagram above shows a very auspicious arrangement for a desk top ensuring that all business dealings are successful.

This is a good desk-top arrangement without too much clutter.

Square (see pages 16–19) covering the surface. To your left is education and learning, your right is governed by helpful people, the area directly before you is the sector of self-knowledge and career prospects and this is the area in which you will do most of your work. The precise centre of the desk relates to your health, to its left is the sector of heritage, and to its right is the sector of creativity. The furthest left hand corner governs wealth, the far centre fame and reputation, while the far right deals with relationships of all kinds, business and personal.

Now you can personalise your work surface by placing photographs of loved ones in your relationship area (Square 2) or family area (Square 3), a small bowl, some coins (as provided with this book) or a healthy plant in your money area (Square 4), and something yellow or representing the Element Earth in your area of knowledge (Square 8). A desk lamp with a curved stem is better than an angular one as this helps beneficial *chi* flow around your work space. If you achieve a harmonious work-top, good fortune is sure to follow.

A skylight provides healthy natural light, but it should be covered if it causes too much glare.

A curved screen increases the flow of *chi* and is a useful partition, separating the office from the rest of the home.

A healthy plant in the money or career areas will aid prosperity.

Drawers and cupboards prevent harmful clutter from accumulating on the desk-top.

The View from the Window

The basic rule behind this is simplicity itself: a good view is good *feng-shui.* A good view not only increases the value of your home, but it also encourages excellent *chi* to enter your dwelling. However, if your property does not possess a good view, there are several *feng-shui* remedies to help you out.

The windows are considered to be the 'eyes' of the home. If you look out on to a blank wall, *feng-shui* practice suggests that a windowbox could help to improve the view. Alternatively, you could buy a stained glass kit and create your own very personal view.

A view of ugly buildings or an untidy back garden can cause unhappiness, so to counter this effect pay close attention to your windows and their surroundings. Attractive curtains do not have to be expensive and with a little imagination you can create a wonderful effect with drapes, swags and colour to draw attention away from the view outside.

Chinese tradition states that North-facing windows need to feature strong *yang* colours, otherwise the ladies of the house may suffer from menstrual problems. This is because women are governed by *yin,* as is the direction North. In addition, North is also associated with the Element Water so this is the connection with bodily fluids.

On the other hand, a South-facing window needs an overhang of some sort, otherwise domestic arguments will be a feature of home life. This is because the South is governed by the Fire Element and therefore things can get heated if too much Fire enters the home through the window.

Net curtains, blinds and other forms of window screening are vital, simply because you don't want strangers prying into your affairs.

Negative Factors

Care must be taken, however, with venetian blinds because there is a possibility that the slats will create harmful 'secret arrows'.

If you detect 'secret arrows' entering your home through a window, from a view of corners, lamp-posts, rooftops and aerials, place a strong, healthy potted plant on the window-sill to ward them off.

From a *feng-shui* point of view, a window that opens outwards is better than one that doesn't allow air in. Two windows that open are better than one as this allows cross-ventilation to occur.

It is very important to replace cracked or broken windows as soon as possible as these can cause eye strain, headaches and general health problems for you.

Attractive curtains and a well-planted windowbox help to soften the effects of sha chi *caused by the sharp corners of the rooftops, aerial, satellite dish and lamp-post in the unplesant view from this window.*

Single Room Living

If you live in a studio apartment, bedsit or any other type of one-room dwelling, the method of putting *feng-shui* into practice can be quite difficult as you need to find room for every activity within a single space. Space is the operative word here; a small area will be much more difficult to arrange since the individual sectors will tend to encroach upon each other.

The best shapes for a studio flat are rectangular and L-shapes. While your flat is essentially an empty space, it does contain areas that are considered to be *yin* and *yang*. The *yang* portions are those in line with the door and windows. The *yin* areas are those which are out of direct line. The *yin* areas are best for the placement of the bed and the dining table. The *yang* areas are more suitable for working and living areas.

The Eight Point Method (see page 18) can be employed in any space, large or small. This will give you the eight all important areas which will need to be balanced out.

The rules about the best Direction for the front door (see page 24) should be followed regarding your flat, but you must also take into account the main door of the building itself, although the Direction of the front door to your flat will take precedence.

The Sleeping Area

The most important piece of furniture is your bed. Use a folding screen, a wardrobe, a cabinet or chest of drawers to separate the sleeping area from the rest of the room. It is also important to keep it out of sight of the doorway. Avoid placing the bed in an area that boxes it in on three sides because this may cause you to have sleepless nights.

Never keep filing cabinets or indeed anything work-related in your screened-off sleeping area because if you do you will soon feel as if you are overwhelmed by work and have no free time to yourself. If you already work in your 'bedroom', then rearrange things so that work occupies the living area rather than the sleeping area.

The rest of the furniture should now be arranged to complement the bed and dining areas which are the two absolute necessities of the room. As the dining table may double up as a worktop, the money sector would be a good position for it.

Further Advice

The rules about piles of junk and general clutter are even more important when you only have one room to live in. A little mess is inevitable, but when it sits there for months on end it can become a depressing influence and can even effect the health. So remember to keep things neat and tidy, and that means having sufficient storage for all your bits and pieces (but don't store them under the bed or you'll have a restless night's sleep).

You can increase your sense of well-being by hanging a wind-chime by the door or window, or by placing a healthy plant or colourful rugs or pictures in relevant sectors.

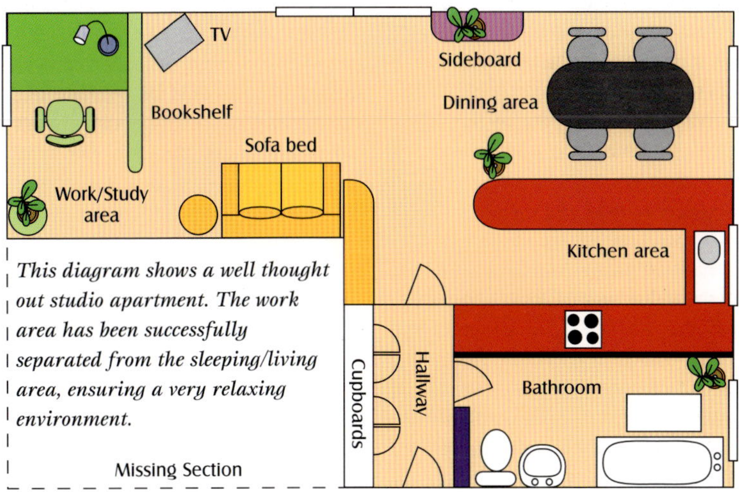

This diagram shows a well thought out studio apartment. The work area has been successfully separated from the sleeping/living area, ensuring a very relaxing environment.

The Dangers of Clutter

Not all of us are perfect home-makers, indeed, some of us actually like to live in chaos! However, from a *feng-shui* point of view, a disorganized home will lead to a disorganized life.

Feng-shui tradition states that the home breathes like a living organism. The vital force, *chi,* enters the home through doors and windows and should be able to flow unobstructed around the corridors and rooms. However, when this gentle meandering is interrupted by piles of clutter the *chi* stagnates and becomes harmful *sha chi.*

Whereas it is inevitable that some junk is bound to accumulate, it shouldn't be left for long periods because harmful *sha chi* will begin to build up. A pile of unironed clothing or a stack of papers left for a very long time can lead to a difficulty in life which will materialize in the sector of the Magic Square in which the clutter sits. 'Secret arrows' may accumulate and cause harm to you and your family.

A cluttered, messy home may lead to neurosis and terrible worry entering your life. If you do tend to be untidy, then there is probably something wrong with your personal Earth Element and you should ask yourself what you need to feel secure and contented.

Clutter near to the main doorway indicates someone who is resisting change, so new opportunities coming into one's life could be rejected out of hand. A feeling of always struggling uphill through life may also be felt. Alternatively, the clutter could be a subconscious way of barricading yourself inside your home and refusing the world entry into your life.

Clutter under the bed is very bad for peace of mind and the health in general. Store your belongings somewhere else and your physical energy and mental well-being will soon improve.

Anyone with this much clutter is asking for trouble!

If there is a pile of junk that just seems to get bigger, stand in the middle of your home and use the Eight Point Method (see page 18) to reveal the area of life which is most troublesome for you.

Clutter and the Five Elements

A pile of clutter also effects the Five Elements within your home. A cluttered Earth area (centre, North East and South West) points to a tendency to worry too much about yourself and could highlight stomach upsets or problems with the spleen or pancreas.

A pile of clutter in the Metal area (West and North West) points to grief and possibly a 'control freak' attitude. It may also highlight problems with the lungs or large intestine.

Clutter in the North, the Water Element, could lead to hidden feelings and anxieties. Complications could occur in the kidneys and bladder.

A messy Wood sector (East and South East) causes confusion and indecision. Frustration and fury are problems which can be reflected in the state of the liver and gallbladder.

If the clutter is in the South then the Element Fire is afflicted. This could lead to volatility of emotions and troubles in affairs of the heart. The immune system, the heart and the small intestine may also be troubled.

FENG-SHUI REMEDIES

Cure 1: *Try to cut down on the amount of clutter in your home by increasing the amount of storage space if necessary.*

Cure 2: *If you are not keen on the minimalist approach, try alternating your favourite ornaments, rather than having them all on display at the same time.*

Cure 3: *Drawers and cupboards are perfect for storage and prevent too much clutter from accumulating.*

One final point.....TIDY UP!

Too many dark colours are bad *feng-shui.* Some lighter *yin* shades should be introduced to balance things out.

Cluttered surfaces cause *sha chi* to accumulate and could lead to bad health.

Chairs should not be positioned with their backs to a window because it causes a subconcious feeling of unease.

Too many loud patterns on furnishings is not conducive to relaxation.

Index